HOW THEY
LIVED

A PLAINS INDIAN
WARRIOR

ROBIN MAY

Illustrated by
Mark Bergin

ROURKE ENTERPRISES INC.
Vero Beach, Florida 32964

Text © 1988 Rourke Enterprises Inc.
PO Box 3328, Vero Beach, Florida 32964

Printed in Belgium.

Library of Congress Cataloging-in-Publication Data

May, Robin.
    A Plains Indian warrior/Robin May; illustrated by Mark Bergin.
        p.   cm. – (How they lived)
    Bibliography: p.
    Includes index.
    Summary: Describes how Native Americans such as the Sioux and
Cheyenne lived before the white man came and destroyed that way of
life.
    ISBN 0–86592–147–4
    1. Indians of North America – Great Plains – Juvenile literature.
[1. Indians of North America – Great Plains.]   I. Bergin, Mark, ill.
II. Title.   III. Series: How they lived (Vero Beach, Fla.)
E78.G73M388 1988
978′.00497 – dc19   87–38306
                                                                   CIP
                                                                    AC

CONTENTS

THE FIRST AMERICANS

The Indian warrior sat as still as a statue on his horse, looking down at the Plains below him. He could see his own camp – a small group of tepees huddled together where about thirty families lived. In a clearing he saw a young Indian boy practicing his horsemanship, which involved trying to mount a pony while it was running at full speed. The boy tugged on the mane, but then lost his grip and fell. If he was to become a warrior he would have to learn to do this with ease.

As the Indian looked into the distance he noticed a long line of wagon trains slowly moving across the landscape. He had never seen so many before. Were they friends or enemies?

The Indians were the first Native Americans. Their ancestors traveled from Asia into North America about 30,000 years ago, crossing the Bering Strait into what is now Alaska. They were given their name by mistake. The explorer Christopher Columbus thought he had reached India in 1492 when he landed on an island in the West Indies, so he named all the inhabitants of the area Indians! At this time, there were only about a million Indians in what is now the United States.

By the eighteenth century, many different tribes had settled in America. Some tribes traveled to the area between the Mississippi River and the Rocky Mountains. This was known as the Great Plains. Plains Indians include tribes such as the Sioux, Comanche, Kiowa, Arapaho, Blackfoot, Cheyenne and the Crow.

A young Indian boy learning the skills of horsemanship.

Ancestors of the first Indians traveled from Asia into North America, across the Bering Strait.

THE DOG DAYS

Before the eighteenth century there were hardly any Indian tribes living on the Great Plains. Indians really needed horses to move around, and as yet there were no horses on the Plains. The few Indians that did attempt to live in this area were often driven off by the terrible droughts.

Without horses, Indians used dogs to pull their possessions when they were traveling. The dogs dragged sleds made from tent poles. These sleds were called *travois* by the French Canadian explorers who saw them. The poles of the sleds were short, as the dogs were not strong enough to drag longer poles. Therefore, the tents that the Indians built at this time were low.

Some Indians were forced onto the Plains as they fled from enemies in the east. Others, who lived and farmed on the edge of the Plains, strayed onto them in search of buffalo – their main food. They hunted buffalo on foot as best they could. The easiest way was to drive the buffalo off a cliff. The more families that joined in the better.

Below   *This map shows the position of the Plains and the Rocky Mountains.*

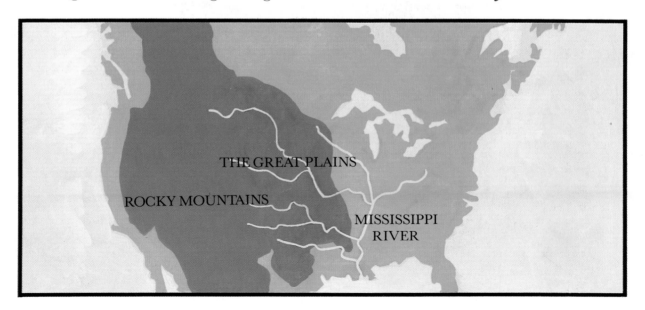

THE GREAT PLAINS

ROCKY MOUNTAINS

MISSISSIPPI RIVER

THE COMING OF THE HORSE

In 1540, Spaniards from Mexico had come to the Plains in search of gold. They were the first to bring horses to the area. Some horses escaped from this expedition, while others escaped from the small settlements built by the Spaniards. Yet, it was a very long time before horses were a common sight. Eventually, horses were traded, and the Indians quickly realized how this animal would transform their lives. Instead of staying on the edge of the Plains, they could now ride onto them and form settlements.

In just a short time, Plains Indian warriors became excellent horseback riders. The Comanche warriors practiced hanging from the neck of their horse while it sped along. They

became so skilled, that they went into battle in this way, shielded from flying arrows by their horse.

Every warrior had his own war horse, which he prized more highly than anything else he owned. A warrior did not use his horse every day, usually only on special occasions, such as going into battle or during a buffalo hunt.

Horse stealing from other tribes scattered around the Plains became a great sport for the Indian warriors. A successful horse thief was regarded with almost as much admiration as a brave fighter in battle. Horses were often given as presents in the tribe. A young warrior would give a horse to the father of the girl he wished to marry — it was known as a *brideprice*.

A Comanche warrior riding into battle, skillfully shielded by his horse.

Indian warriors had the task of breaking in the new wild horses.

BUFFALO HUNTING

The forests and grassy prairies of the Plains were perfect for the Indians' way of life. They discovered that everything they needed to live comfortably could be found there.

The buffalo was the most important of all animals to the Indians because it gave them food, shelter and clothing. Every part of its body was used in some way. Knives and arrowheads were made from the bones, water buckets from the stomach, and hides were used to make their shoes known as *moccasins*.

Naturally, buffalo hunting was important – and very exciting. Before Indians had horses, it was a slow and dangerous business on foot. A number of families would surround a small herd and some of the warriors would dress up in wolfskins, as buffalo were not afraid of wolves. In this way, they could creep nearer to the buffalo and attack them with spears and arrows.

The coming of the horse made buffalo hunting a thrilling occasion. Indian warriors could race in and out of herds on their well-trained horses, shooting arrows at the animal. Young Indian boys sometimes helped in the hunt because it was thought to be good training for later life. They would ride with the

warriors on their small ponies, without stirrups or saddles. The warriors often gave the buffalo meat to a widow who had recently lost her husband, or to a man who was too old to hunt.

After the hunt, the warriors did the heavy work of butchering, but it was the women of the tribe who cut the animal up, to make use of every part of it. All Indians respected the huge buffalo. They hunted it because their way of life depended on it, as well as for the sport.

Indian women treating buffalo hides.

Warriors hunting buffalo on the Plains.

THE TRIBE

The Indians' way of life was governed by customs, rather than by set laws. The chief or chiefs of the tribe were not all-powerful figures as they are sometimes depicted. They did not give orders, but simply offered advice. There were different chiefs for different purposes, such as war chiefs, civil chiefs and medicine men. The chiefs of a tribe would meet regularly to talk about tribal matters. The Cheyenne tribe had a Council of forty-four, consisting of forty chiefs and four old man chiefs. They were very fair. If a new rule was to be passed, they asked the opinion of all the tribe before passing it.

Because Plains Indians were a warrior group of nations, the war chiefs who led the warrior societies, were very important and highly respected. A successful warrior could become a chief if he was elected by the whole tribe. But he could also lose the honor if the tribe lost confidence in him as a wise leader.

An Indian warrior was allowed a great deal of freedom, but bad behavior was frowned upon. Occasionally, if fighting started among his own people, the chief would intervene by carrying sacred peace pipes to the people concerned, in a hope that the fighting would stop. If, more seriously, a murder was committed, the tribe would persuade the killer and his family to give horses and other goods to the victim's family to stop a feud from beginning. Really bad behavior could also result in a warrior being driven into exile. The tribe always came first.

Left *The chiefs of the tribe often met to discuss tribal matters.*

Right *Chief Sitting Bull of the Sioux was both a warrior and a medicine man.*

A Warrior's Home

The Plains Indians lived in tents called lodges or *tepees*. These were supported by three or four strong poles, along with some smaller poles that were tied together at the top. Seventeen or more tanned buffalo hides were needed to cover a tepee, and the hides were then staked to the ground, for the Plains winds were very fierce. Two women could build a tepee very quickly, and it could be dismantled easily if there was any fear of danger.

A tepee was waterproof, and in good weather a flap was opened to let air in. There were also two smoke-flaps, to let out the smoke from the fire, which was in the center of the tepee. These flaps could be closed to stop drafts. Cooking was usually

The inside of a tepee was warm and comfortable.

done outside the tepee, as long as the weather was fine. In the early days, when Indians had only dogs to rely on, their tepees were much smaller and not so elaborate.

The tepee was not just somewhere for the Indians to live. Because it was circular it was more than a home, for the circle was a sacred shape in Indian religion. Indian women decorated their tepees with pictures of battles, visions and other designs. The entrance to the tepee always faced east, as this is the direction that

A young Blackfoot warrior outside a decorated tepee.

the sun rises in the morning.

Buffalo skins were used for bedding, and the floor of the tepee was also lined with some buffalo hides to keep out the cold. Women made backrests for each end of the bed for extra comfort. All in all, the Indian tepee was much more comfortable than the average settler's sod house, which was made of earth and grass.

FAMILY LIFE

Family life was very important to the Indians. However, Plains Indian women were not generally looked upon as equals by the Indian warriors. While they led an exciting life hunting and fighting, the women worked long, hard hours looking after the camp. Although the warriors killed the buffalo, it was the women who treated the hides.

Generally, the Plains Indians had happy marriages. In fact, it was the women who tended to choose their husbands. No Indian women would

For most young Indian children, camp life was happy and carefree.

ever think of marrying a warrior until he had proved himself in battle. When a young couple fell in love, a warrior would often sit outside the girl's tepee and play his flute.

Among the Sioux there was no marriage ceremony as such; a new wife would just take her belongings to her warrior's tepee. However, in other tribes weddings were celebrated with feasts and exchanges of presents.

The Sioux warrior was quite a kind husband. In the morning he would sometimes brush his wife's long black hair and paint her face

A married couple of the Kiowa tribe.

with red and yellow dyes. A warrior could have several wives, if he could afford them. Everybody lived together in the family's tepee.

Children in most tribes led a very happy life, and their parents often spoiled them. However, a child who cried too much had to be cured, for the noise might give away the camp's position to an enemy. Some mothers took their children outside in their *cradleboards* and left them hanging on a bush until they stopped crying. Children soon learned their lesson!

All the different generations of the tribe had a part to play in camp life. Grandparents often helped out by amusing the children while their parents were busy. They would recount tribal tales and in this way the Indians' history and way of life was passed on to the next generation.

An Indian woman with her baby in a cradleboard.

17

RELIGION AND RITUAL

Plains Indian warriors lived close to nature. The earth was regarded as their "mother," as it helped them to survive. They did not think of the land as being owned by anyone as the white settlers believed. You could not buy it because it was part of nature – like the sun and the sky. It was a sacred trust. The land was a central part of their religion, as was "medicine."

Medicine was the "spirit" that protected a warrior in daily life and in battle. Strong medicine was thought to help a warrior greatly. Medicine men were both priests and doctors. They learned to cure sick people and to heal warriors' wounds with special plants and herbs. Many of their findings are now accepted by American doctors.

All Indian warriors felt close to the spirit world. Some even took part in a religious ceremony known as the Sun Dance. This was an important ritual because, as one warrior explained, "all living creatures and plants receive their life from the sun." In the Sun Dance, a warrior would cut down a thin tree and place it in the center of the camp. Then, when ready, he would drive wooden hooks into his flesh and attach a leather thong from these hooks to the tree. As dawn broke he would dance around the tree, and, in a trance-like state, manage to pull the hooks from his skin. The painful scars from this ritual were displayed with pride.

Sitting Bull of the Sioux, a war chief and a medicine man, endured the Sun Dance just before the famous Battle of the Little Big Horn (known as Custer's Last Stand) in 1876. During the ritual he had a vision of white soldiers falling into the Sioux camp upside-down. This meant that the soldiers would lose the battle. A few hours later this vision came true, for Custer and his men were defeated.

Most warriors had a sacred place, such as a mountain, that they often visited. Here they would sit in the hope of seeing a vision, but few could have seen one as sensational as Sitting Bull's.

Right *The Sun Dance was an important religious ritual performed by brave warriors in honor of the sun.*

18

A Warrior's Clothes

For most Plains Indians, war was a way of life. All young warriors dreamed of winning fame in battle, and on such occasions they wore really fine clothes. These were known as their war costumes, and they also might have been worn at other special ceremonies. Some were like

An Indian warrior in his elaborate war costume, holding a coup stick. Everyday clothes were simpler, but just as colorful, often decorated with hundreds of tiny beads.

military uniforms – they showed how important a warrior was, or that he belonged to a particular religious group.

An Indian's war shirt was highly decorated, sometimes with the hair of an enemy. Certain beads and quills represented awards for bravery in war, and some shirts actually had battle pictures painted on them. However, most important to warriors were their medicine shirts, which they believed to have special powers. This sometimes had unhappy results – a warrior would

Plains Indians wore shoes called moccasins made from buffalo hide.

This Blackfoot warrior, called Bird Rattler, displays his war bonnet.

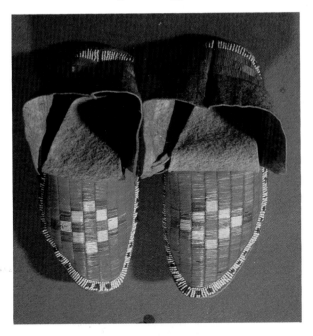

go into battle thinking that his medicine shirt would deflect bullets, which unfortunately it could not. Some warriors went into battle bare-chested except for a few medicine signs painted on them for protection.

Some warriors wore elaborate headdresses known as "war bonnets," while others wore just one or two feathers in their hair. An eagle feather could only be worn by those who were especially brave. Their war horses also had special signs painted on them, which were linked to the warrior's religion.

21

A Warrior's Weapons

Before the white man came, Indians fought with bows and arrows, spears and clubs. Later, they used firearms and spears tipped with metal. However, many warriors went on using bows and arrows for some time, as the first guns were hard to load and not very accurate.

The Plains Indians were skilled bowmen. Their arrowheads were carved from bone or stone, until the white traders supplied metal ones.

Indians liked to shoot within a 100-yard (approximately 90-meter) range, but the best bowmen could shoot farther. Clubs, knives and *tomahawks* were also used, along with small shields decorated with medicine signs and feathers.

An important part of a young warrior's training was to perform a *coup*. No youth was thought to be a man until he had carried out this deed of valor. Young warriors would have to go into battle unarmed and, if they successfully touched the enemy and returned uninjured, they would gain the respect of the whole tribe. It was also considered courageous to touch the enemy with a "coup stick" and escape, rather than kill him.

It was during the late Indian Wars from the 1860s to 1890s that bows gradually gave way to rifles and pistols. At first, the possessor of a rifle was envied, but later all warriors had one. But only a few had the necessary training to use rifles really well. Traders supplied guns, often illegally, knowing they would be used to fight white men. In the final

Indian Wars heavy artillery was used by white soldiers. The Indians could not defend themselves against such weapons.

Left *Warriors sometimes went into battle armed only with a coup stick. To touch the enemy with this stick and escape was highly regarded.*

Above *In the 1860s white traders began to supply firearms to the Indians in exchange for goods. Soon the bow and arrow was out-of-date.*

23

FOOD AND DRINK

As we have seen, the most important food for the Plains Indians was buffalo meat. It was very tasty and nourishing – even little children were given pieces of it to suck. Every part of the buffalo that could be eaten was eaten! Boiling and roasting were the main methods for cooking the meat.

For the long winter months, buffalo meat was dried and stored.

Buffalo meat, the Indians most important food, was usually roasted on a large makeshift spit.

Sometimes it was beaten into a powder and mixed with berries and fat to make *pemmican*. This rich food could be kept for a long time in containers called *parfleches*, which were made from rawhide.

Indians also ate deer meat, rabbits and antelopes when they could catch them, and some tribes enjoyed fish. Other tribes did not approve of eating fish. Vegetables that were eaten included wild peas, onions and radishes. There were also many wild fruits on the Plains.

Gradually, white settlers became interested in the Plains – they wanted to develop the land for their own use. They started building railroads, and fed their workers on the buffalo from the region. They killed so many that it left the Indians very short of food. It was a way of forcing the Indians to leave the land they had lived on for many, many years.

Unfortunately, by the end of the 1870s the most popular drink for Indians was whiskey, which was supplied by white traders. This drink was usually of very poor quality and greatly harmed the Indians who were not used to alcohol. But there were always traders who would sell it to the Indians however much the authorities tried to stop them.

A colorful rawhide container called a parfleche was used to store dried buffalo meat.

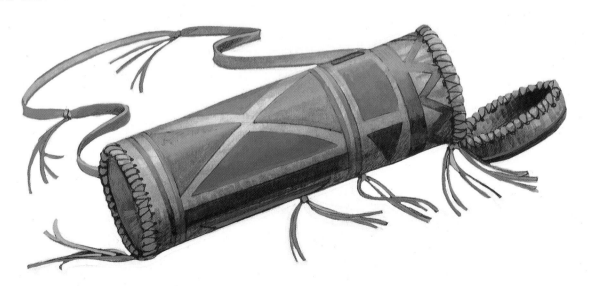

THE INDIAN WARS

There was little trouble on the Plains between early Americans and Indians until the 1850s. Gradually wagon trains took settlers across to the Pacific coast, but the Indians still did not feel threatened. Some white men actually lived with the Indians, and others visited them.

From the 1850s things changed. Suddenly the Indians were "in the way," especially when the new settlers found that the Plains were good farming land. Many thousands of people poured onto them from the eastern United States and Europe. The old free life of the Plains Indians was doomed.

There were far more Americans on the Plains now than Indians, and they were better armed. Railroads were also built, which could rush soldiers to the Plains in times of conflict. Yet, under great warriors like Sitting Bull and Crazy Horse of the Sioux, Quanah Parker of the Comanche, and Dull Knife and Two Moons of the Cheyenne, they fought bravely against larger, better-armed white forces. At the Battle of Little Big Horn, Indians from the Sioux, Cheyenne and Arapaho tribes, defeated General Custer and 265 of his seventh cavalry. This was a great victory, but setbacks were soon to follow.

One of the main problems of the Plains Indian warriors was that they could not fight in winter. It was all they could do to survive, with the buffalo almost wiped out by white hunters.

This painting, called Watching the Wagons, *shows some of the first American settlers arriving on the Great Plains.*

During the Indian wars, warriors had to fight against better-armed white forces.

THE END OF THE OLD LIFE

By the start of the 1880s most Plains Indians had been forced onto reservations set aside by the United States government. Some tribes, like the brave Northern Cheyenne, escaped and tried to get home. Most Indians were sent back to their reservations, but the Cheyenne had suffered so much that Americans started to recognize the plight of the Indians. It was decided that they could stay in their Montana home.

Chief Big Foot lies dead in the snow after the battle at Wounded Knee.

1880: A Sioux reservation. Canvas tents were supplied in place of the tepee.

Others were less lucky. Reservations were usually on land that the white people did not want. Plains Indian warriors knew nothing of farming, and the land they were given was often unfit for farming anyway.

The last Indian War was in 1890. The Sioux tribe heard a report from a holy man that white people would vanish from the west and the buffalo would return. Although the Sioux were at peace, some felt they had to act. A final battle was fought in the snow at Wounded Knee, leaving many men, women and children dead. The Indian Wars were finally over.

After the wars, life was harder for Plains Indians. They were forbidden to be real Indians; their religion was called heathen; and they lost their lands (much of which was stolen dishonestly). They were not even allowed to wear their hair long.

A few joined Wild West shows, the best being run by Buffalo Bill Cody. He liked the Indian warriors and they respected him. Together they toured the United States, Britain and Europe. It was better than being trapped on a reservation.

After the wars, some warriors joined Buffalo Bill's Wild West Show.

TODAY AND TOMORROW

Early in the twentieth century the numbers of Indians in the United States fell so drastically that it seemed this race of proud people would not survive. In the 1930s, President Roosevelt tried to help all Indians become part of a tribe again. They were left to run their own reservations, and more Indians were employed to assist in Indian affairs.

Today, the Indians are no longer a vanishing race, but they still face many problems. Jobs are hard to find, and the prejudice of some people makes matters worse. In the 1970s some young Indians felt so frustrated that they turned to violence to gain equality with the rest of society.

Lawyers have helped Indians to get money for their lost lands, but this only goes a small way toward paying for the loss of a way of life. Some politicians feel that the reservations should be closed, but the Indians – in Canada as well as the United States – fear this would lead to the many different tribes fighting for land. Whatever happens in the future, one thing is for certain – the Plains Indians will survive.

Charlie Red Cloud of the Sioux. Today, the Plains Indians are no longer a vanishing race, although most still live on reservations.

GLOSSARY

Artillery Extremely large mounted guns, such as cannons.

Customs Traditional habits of a society or group.

Equality Being equal to, and being treated in the same way as, other people.

Generation A single stage in a family's history.

Heathen A type of religion that is unlike traditional religions.

Native Americans The only people living in much of North America before Europeans came. They are also called Indians.

Opinion What a person thinks or believes about a subject.

Prejudice An unfair opinion or feeling about a person or race.

Quills Large feathers from a bird.

Ritual A set way of performing a religious ceremony.

Sacred To be regarded with respect and reverence.

Settlement A small group of people who have settled in a place to live.

Tanning A method of treating an animal skin or hide with vegetable or fish oils to make a softer leather.

Tomahawk A small axe.

Trance When the mind is in a dream-like state.

Transform To change something a great deal.

Vision A picture or dream in the mind.

MORE BOOKS TO READ

Among the Plains Indians, Lorenz Engel (Lerner, 1970)

Bury My Heart at Wounded Knee, Dee Brown (Holt, 1971)

Indian Chiefs, Russell Freedman (Holiday, 1987)

Indians of the Northern Plains, William K. Powers (Patnam, 1969)

North American Indians, Susan Pardy and Cass R. Sandak (Watts, 1982)

Plains Indians, Jill Hughes (Watt, 1984)

The Plains Indians of North America, Robin May (Rourke, 1987)

The Red Swan: Myths and Tales of the American Indians, John Bierhorst (editor) (Farrar Straus Giraux, 1985)

Tipi: A Center of Native American Life, Charlotte Yue (Knopf, 1983)

INDEX

Picture acknowledgments
The pictures in this book were supplied by the following: Peter Newark's Western Americana 5, 11, 17 (both), 21 (bottom), 23, 27, 28 (bottom) The Robin May Collection 13 (The Smithsonian Institute), 15, 21 (top), 28 (top) Colin Taylor 30. The remaining pictures are from the Wayland Picture Library.